AMAZING FRIENDSHIPS

How to make and keep
good friends the
Friendcraft way

Paul Barrass

Copyright © 2006 Paul Barrass

The moral right of the author has been asserted.

Apart from any fair dealing for the purposes of research or private study, or criticism or review, as permitted under the Copyright, Designs and Patents Act 1988, this publication may only be reproduced, stored or transmitted, in any form or by any means, with the prior permission in writing of the publishers, or in the case of reprographic reproduction in accordance with the terms of licences issued by the Copyright Licensing Agency. Enquiries concerning reproduction outside those terms should be sent to the publishers.

Matador Publishing
9 De Montfort Mews
Leicester LE1 7FW, UK
Email: books@troubador.co.uk
Web: www.troubador.co.uk/matador

ISBN 10: 1 905886 00 4
ISBN 13: 9781905886005

Printed by The Cromwell Press Ltd, Trowbridge, Wilts, UK

Matador is an imprint of Troubador Publuishing Ltd

Table of Contents

Acknowledgments 7

Chapter 1
Introduction to the Friendcraft Way................. 11
    Activity One
    Why Are You Reading This Book? 15

Chapter 2
The Journey into Friendship....................... 19
    Activity Two
    Journeying into Friendship..................... 25

Chapter 3
What Is a Friend?................................ 29
    Activity Three
    What Attracts You to Someone as a Friend? 32

Chapter 4
Being Your Own Best Friend 35
    Activity Four
    Getting to Know You 48

Chapter 5
The Friendcraft Model 51
    Activity Five
    Mapping Your Personal Community 60

Chapter 6
Making Friends 63
    Activity Six
    Making Friends 72

Chapter 7
Cultivating Friendships 75
    Activity Seven
    Deepening Friendships. 82

Chapter 8
Kinds of Friendships 85
    Activity Eight
    Looking at Your Friendships. 92

Chapter 9
False Friends. 95
    Activity Nine
    Disengaging from False Friendships 105

Chapter 10
Boundaries and Structure in Friendships 109
    Activity Ten
    Boundaries in Your Friendships 115

Chapter 11
Mutual Support and Effort. 119
    Activity Eleven
    Reflecting on Your Friendships. 127

Chapter 12
Community and Belonging 131

About the Author. 139

Acknowledgments

A book like this one does not just happen. I would like to acknowledge the kind assistance of the people who believed in my ideas and who helped me to communicate them.

Firstly, my lovely wife, Shirley, who supported me through the writing and editing process.

My close friend and collaborator, Mary Ann Chang, who has been the source of so much inspiration and support in developing the Friendcraft Way.

My editor, Melanie Rigney, for her very professional guidance in matters of form and presentation.

To those people who have warmed the journey of my life with their friendship, I give a sincere thank you. You are too numerous to mention by name, but I treasure the times we have spent together and look forward to much more of your company as we journey on.

I

Introduction to the Friendcraft Way

Activity One
Why Are You Reading This Book?

Friendship is a vitally important subject for us all. The people in our lives have a major impact on our happiness and satisfaction. We may not have much choice about our relatives, but we certainly can choose our friends. Sadly, too many people just allow their "friendships" to grow casually and then become disappointed and disillusioned when things don't work out and people let them down. This happens because they have not used the principles of what I call Friendcraft in making, sustaining, and enhancing their friendships. They have left the development of this vital area of life to the winds of chance.

This book is for anyone who is serious about having good friends in life, and that should be everyone. This is a book that should speak to your heart. This is a book that should speak to your mind. This is a book that may speak to your spirit, for it is about what makes you you. You are a unique and special person. Why would you want to give the gift of your friendship to people who abuse, neglect, or misuse it? And yet, millions of people do this all the time.

Friendship is a very personal thing. Your friendship is something to be valued. It is not something to be casually given away. Nor is it a thing to be taken for granted. You can decide whom to have as friends and how those friendships can develop in ways that will be positive both for you and those you honour with your friendship. I will say more about this in the chapters that follow.

I have spent twenty-five years as a therapist in the British National Health Service working with staff, patients, carers, and others who have failed to make the friendship connection in their lives. I have spent over twenty-five years counselling friends, colleagues, and people from volunteer groups who have similarly failed to appreciate the need to consciously make life-enhancing friendship choices. My experience led me to develop a system that I call Friendcraft. It transformed my life. I recommended it to others, and it transformed their lives, and I finally have been persuaded to recommend it to you. It is my gift to you. I hope it enables you to make life-enhancing choices so that your friendships can be sources of happiness, fulfilment, and joy for you. This comes with understanding the journey of friendship and how the art of Friendcraft can help you be the person you want to be and have the friends you would like to have.

Friendcraft gives us a positive and realistic way of looking at our friendships. It puts you in the driver's seat in making and developing your friendships at whatever level you choose. It is a special and unique system that will enable you to take control in finding, developing, and nurturing those friendships that will become a welcome part of your life.

If you read this book, think about what it contains, and apply its principles, beneficial changes will take place in your life and in the lives of those you influence through your friendships. I believe that you are a special and unique person and that your friendship is one of the most precious gifts that you can bestow.

In this book, we shall look at the concepts and subtleties of the Friendcraft approach. We will talk about the levels of friendship and define who is a close friend as opposed to a casual friend or a social acquaintance or a business acquaintance or somebody with whom we have some important but limited contact. We will look at these layers of friendship and how they add up to make a satisfying and supportive personal community. We will consider how we meet friends and how we allow them into our lives. Sometimes it is a question of whether we have allowed them in or they have intruded for their own purposes. I call people in the latter category false friends and, indeed, we will look at them in detail as well.

We expect different things from our different kinds of friends. For example, if you have a friend you consider a casual friend or acquaintance, somebody with whom you merely exchange a few greetings, you would not be sharing with him or her the important details of major events that are happening in your life except on the most superficial level.

I work with many people, most of whom do not know when it is my birthday. They certainly would not dream of buying me a birthday present any more than I would dream of buying them one. But at a major holiday such as Christmas, they may send me a card and I may send them one with nothing more than a casual greeting inside. With those who are closer friends, I might remember birthdays and share personal news in Christmas cards. But the most intimate and most challenging or even most joyous things I share only with those very few people who form the innermost circle of my very special friends.

We can think of the Friendcraft model of friendships as an archery target, with you as the goal (bull's-eye) surrounded by your most intimate and inner circle of friends, who probably can be numbered on the fingers of one or two hands, at the centre. In concentric rings outward are other kinds of friends, from the close to the casual to the mere acquaintances in your life.

I will give you guidelines and suggestions for deciding the criteria you might like to use in admitting people into closer levels of friendship. Believe me, the choice rests with you.

Exercises

The information and ideas in this book are also presented in Friendcraft workshops. In these workshops, participants are guided in reflecting on their friendships and on changes that would make their lives happier and their friendships more satisfying. Discussions and group activities help the participants acquire understanding and skills to help them in making these changes.

At the end of the chapters are activities I have designed to guide and assist you in looking at your friendships and having more satisfying friendships in your life. You may find it useful to write your responses in a journal or notebook devoted to these exercises and recording your thoughts about your friendships. The time you spend doing these exercises will go a long way in helping you achieve satisfying changes in your friendships, shape your personal community of friends, and have a happier life.

✪ Activity One
Why Are You Reading This Book?

1. Why are you reading this book? What do you want to get out of it?

2. Think about the friendships in your life. What do they mean to you?

3. Are you getting what you want and expect out of your various friendships? What are you giving in return?

4. What are some things about your friendships that you would like to be different?

2

THE JOURNEY INTO FRIENDSHIP

Activity Two
Journeying into Friendship

The journey into friendship begins when two people meet for the first time. I describe this process as a journey in that it has a definite beginning. It starts with people meeting or communicating. It has an ultimate destination at whatever level of friendship you determine you are going to allow that person to reach in your life.

Like many journeys we make in life, this one may not be straight. There may be twists and turns along the way. There may be unexpected delays. There may be stop signs. There may be cancellations of the journey, or you may have to take another route. It may be a journey you set off on only to discover that instead of travelling north, you should have been travelling south. It may be a journey that lasts a lifetime.

A great philosopher said that to travel hopefully is better than to arrive. Some people actually enjoy the journey far more than arriving at a destination. I do not endorse or oppose that school of thought. I merely say that the journey itself is as interesting as arriving at the destination. It depends on how you view journeying. You can see it as mere travel from point A to point B, an inconvenience that interrupts the smooth flow of your life. This is how some people see their friendships.

There are people who want instant results, instant travel. They would love to step onto the Star Trek transporter device in the sense of a friendship—a button is pressed, and zap! they have an instant friend. But real life is not like that. Real life is a slower, more uncertain, sometimes almost organic process, very similar to walking a path toward a mountain. In the distance, the mountain may look small, but as you approach it, the mountain grows larger. You start to see things you didn't notice before. You adjust your course accordingly.

Another reason that I describe the process of making and cultivating friendships as a journey is because sensible people make preparations before they set out on a journey. They do not just say, "I will travel from New York to Beijing" and then walk out their front door, leaving their house unlocked, and hail a taxi and set off without any money in their pockets. In some journeys, people encounter unexpected emergencies and even expected difficulties along the way. Just as the sensible person carefully considers and plans when taking a journey, so we should do when choosing friends and admitting people into the innermost areas of our lives.

Some books are written on the assumption that people are slightly gullible and rather foolish. I do not believe my readers to be foolish or gullible. I know that I am communicating with people who carefully consider the choices they make in their lives. They make adequate preparations for the journeys they have to take. The journey of friendship is no different than any other journey.

While we are on the journey, we need to review our progress. Are we heading in the direction we intended? Do we need to rest for a while and take stock of the situation? For example, if I were going to walk across the whole of the county in which I live, it would take me about three days. I would not want to do that without taking rest and refreshment and considering my feet. Were I to keep doggedly on, I might collapse of thirst or tiredness, or my feet might become blistered and of very little use to me.

I would say to anyone taking the journey into friendship that there may be moments when you need to pause, reflect, and consider the direction in which you are going. Is the journey still worthwhile? Do you have adequate resources to complete it? Is your plan a good plan? Does it need revision? What is the journey doing to you? Are you making sacrifices in terms of your well-being and peace of mind that are costing you more than the destination is worth?

Have you been to a well-kept garden, a garden whose beauty takes your breath away? It did not happen by accident. There was a design from the start. There is a plan for the future. The garden has been nurtured. Things have grown naturally, but they have also been planned. Weeds have been removed, paths have been laid, and water has been brought where it needed to be at appropriate times.

If you look at the beauty of nature, there are wonderful scenes that grow without the need of the gardener's hand. But you will not see all the different elements brought together that you would in a well-kept garden. In the cultivated garden, there may be flowers, vegetables, and fruits from different parts of this wide and diverse planet.

And so it can be with our friendships. We may live in particular place and be part of a particular culture, but by applying the skills of Friendcraft we can choose to enrich our lives with friendships with people from other places and other ways of life. This is the difference between the Friendcraft approach and the free-floating attitude of "I can just make friends with people I happen to meet and I don't need to think about it." If you abandoned your garden to the vagaries of nature and just hoped that everything would be hunky-dory and that the rain would fall, the sun would shine, and the wind would blow, would your garden be exactly as you left it? I don't think so.

People do that when they have despaired or given up gardening or chosen to conduct their gardens in a so-called natural way. What happens is that the wildflowers that many of us call weeds grow up and choke out everything else.

And so it is with people who just free-float through their friendships, letting people into their lives and closest acquaintance willy-nilly. If they are lucky, they end up with beautiful wildflowers. If they are not lucky, they end up with a garden of thorns and strangleweed. And how does the rose, even the wild rose, bloom amid that?

Friendcraft, like any other craft or art, is something to be thought about, practised, and cultivated. It is an approach that has a model and a practical application. You have to think about it. You have to have an idea of what you want to create before you set out to create it. You cannot just let things happen and expect that whatever results will suit your likes and needs. That rarely works.

Friendcraft provides a series of reflections that you can do with respect to how and why you admit people into friendship. Once you have carefully considered these concepts, you will find that you can make conscious choices and that you will naturally review them as time goes on.

How many of you sleepwalk on the job? How many of you sleepwalk when shopping? I suspect very few. You are making conscious decisions. Then why on earth would you sleepwalk into friendships? I have searched my heart on this matter, and it begs belief that people will entrust one of the most important things they will ever have in their lives to chance.

This said, it is true that people may meet by chance and a great friendship may develop. For example, one of my best and most intimate friends and I met at a meeting. Volunteers were called for to produce a show. My friend at the back of the room and I at the front stood up and said we would help. We had not met before that night. We had never cooperated on any project before, but with a brisk handshake and a promise to meet the following week, having foolishly made the offer and been left standing alone with nobody else to assist, we agreed to take on the task together. Our friendship developed in the course of working on this project and later broadened into many more areas of our lives. We have become very firm friends and have increased the depths of our involvement as the years have progressed.

But the development of this friendship was not as much by chance as one might first think. Working together on projects is a good way to develop meaningful friendships, much more so than chatting up people over drinks. Later in the book, we will talk about this and other ways to encourage the development of lasting and life-enhancing friendships.

Just this very morning, I spoke with my friend by phone as I was sitting in one country and he was in another, thousands of miles away. Distance and not having been together for a while did not keep us from expressing our friendship. He asked me how the book was going, and I asked him how things were with his family and in an organization in which we are both members. This is something I shall deal with later in the book: how to develop and sustain friendships over long distances. In this modern world, that is something that is also worth considering.

✪ Activity Two
Journeying into Friendship

1. Reflect on what makes you unique: your talents, special contributions, and things you have done in life. Which of these things would you like your friends to know about you? Which of these things might you choose to share with people you meet to help them get to know you?

2. Imagine you are travelling on a journey and will be meeting new people and making new friends. What kinds of people would you like to meet along the way? What kinds of people would you like to have as travelling companions?

3

WHAT IS A FRIEND?

Activity Three
What Attracts You to Someone as a Friend?

We have talked about friendship as a journey and cultivating friendships as a gardener would carefully plan and tend a garden. Now, let's look at what a friend is and what being a friend means.

There are two things people mention when they talk about their friends. One is liking their friends, liking to be with them, liking to do things together, and talking with them about things that matter. The other thing people mention is caring about their friends and being willing to invest their time to help them.

But we all know that we care more about some of our friends than others and that we can count on some friends when we need help while others will be nowhere to be seen. These are the things that go into defining the levels of friendship.

There is a difference between having a friend and being a friend. If you are a close friend with someone, then that person's happiness and well-being are important to you. You are willing to invest some of your time and energy in seeing that the person's life is happy and in helping out if he or she needs it. There is a commitment and willingness to help implied when we talk about "being a friend."

Then there are casual friends who don't mean a whole lot to you. You enjoy their company, but you aren't willing to go very far out of your way for them. You are happy to share the good times together, but you don't want to spend much if any of your time helping them.

The levels of friendship represent different degrees of sharing and caring. There are some people with whom we share important things in our lives. There are those with whom we share only lighter social experiences. There are others with whom we only share a hobby. There are friends we care deeply about and would drop whatever we were doing to help them, even though we may not see them often. There are casual friends we may enjoy seeing daily but do not feel committed to helping with their problems.

A very good friend of mine recently lost a dear teacher and mentor whom she had not seen more than perhaps a couple times a year in recent years. Yet, his passing left a tremendous gap in her life. Had he called on her for assistance, she would have dropped everything to help him. During the years of their teacher-student relationship, she did things for him ranging from helping to paint his home to heading up special projects on his behalf. He likewise had a deep commitment to her. His door was always open if she needed to talk with him. He extended exceptional hospitality to her, from personally making home-cooked meals she could enjoy when visiting to seeing that she had a place to stay nearby. He taught her everything from how to cook the dishes of his homeland to the most profound subjects of his personal philosophy. They shared many hours. Their friendship was deep. Life took them their separate ways but their friendship and mutual commitment did not fade.

We will talk more about lasting friendships at a later stage. In our modern world, there may well be dear friends who live at distances very remote from you. You still may care about them deeply and have great interest in their welfare and well-being. You do not have to be with friends 24/7 for the friendship to be deep and enduring.

In the next chapter, I will like to introduce you to someone very important in your life. In fact, this person is the best and most enduring friend you can ever have. It is you.

✪ Activity Three
What Attracts You to Someone as a Friend?

1. Reflect on the qualities you like your friends to have.

2. When you meet someone you would consider having as a friend, what qualities in that person do you respond to? What makes you feel that person would make a good friend for you?

3. Imagine you are meeting for the first time someone with whom you really feel you want to be friends. Why do you feel this way? What is that person like? How does he or she talk, move, make eye contact, and so on?

4

BEING YOUR OWN BEST FRIEND

Activity Four
Getting to Know You

Making the conscious decision to be your own best friend is one of the most important aspects of Friendcraft. For how can you make life-enhancing decisions about admitting others into your life when you are not fully aware of what a good friend you have in yourself? Many of us shy away from making a good friend of ourselves because there are things in our lives that we feel will prevent us from doing this. But is it not important that you care about your own happiness, well-being, health, and development? Surely, the most life-enhancing choices you can make at the beginning of the journey into friendship are the choices you make about yourself.

Let's try an exercise. Tomorrow morning when you get up, look into your mirror. Look into the face that is looking back at you and say to yourself, "I am a special and unique person. The world is better for me being here. I have much to contribute on the journey into friendship." It is quite true. You are a special and unique person. You do have a lot to contribute. There are people in this world who would enjoy being your friend.

Why not take time to make those life-enhancing decisions about your own health, well-being, and happiness that will make it so much easier for you to engage others and for them to feel comfortable engaging you? Why not take the time to really get to know you?

We can't all be famous, rich, powerful, brilliant, athletic, or any other of the things people often wish they were. But we can all engage with other people in activities that recognize and nurture us as unique human beings.

You may say to me, "There are things I don't like about myself. I am too thin, too tall, too short, too black, too white, too red, too pink with green spots…you know…I wish I were somebody else." I have one question for you. Why?

You are who you are. And there is nothing wrong with that, but you can make some life-enhancing choices about your health and about your body that may help in increasing your sense of well-being and happiness. For example, some of us could do with losing a few pounds. I include myself in that.

Life has dealt you a hand, a physical shape, a gender, a place where you were born, and a place where you live at the moment. Becoming comfortable with who you are, what you have achieved, and what you can contribute through the art of Friendcraft will bring you a degree of serenity and satisfaction. Others will sense this and be drawn to it. They will notice these qualities in you.

Think about it. When you feel happy, it shows in your face. Even people who barely know you begin to respond to you in a positive manner. How much easier will it be to open meaningful communication with people and to start to use the skills of Friendcraft if you have a positive attitude toward yourself!

You can take the most famous painting in the world and hang a dust sheet over it and parade through the streets of any major city in the world and no one will know it is there. But take the cover off, and everybody can see the beauty that lies within. Isn't it a tragedy that so many of us conceal our true beauty and undervalue or dismiss the special and unique contributions that we make during our lifetimes? Others can come to appreciate and regard us in a much more positive way if they see our true worth.

So, let us start to make friends with ourselves. Let us start to be comfortable with who we are and the situation that we are in. Yes, we may work to improve certain things about ourselves, our physical appearance to some extent, our education, or our promotion prospects at work. Yes, there is nothing wrong with any of that. But let's start the process of becoming our own best friend, of becoming comfortable with who we are and what we can achieve. Be happy to see the face that looks back at you, even if that face looks older or greyer or has a few more pounds than in an ideal world. We do not live in an ideal world; we live in this world. And we need to make the most of what we've got and to make the vital preparations within ourselves to begin the journey into friendship.

Someone with whom I once worked was convinced that because she was not more than five feet tall, taller people did not take her seriously. She had allowed her height to become a major factor in how she saw other people and in how she saw herself. She did not see herself as a special and unique person with a contribution to make or as somebody who could form friendships with people who were taller than she was. Once when a rather shy tall gentleman asked her out for a drink, she rebuffed his invitation firmly and he never asked her out again since he took her refusal seriously. She confided to me that she regretted this since she liked him and was attracted to him and knew that he liked her. We talked about this on several occasions and she disclosed more and more to me. I asked her to consider reflecting on whether there were things in her life that were stopping her from being happy with who she was.

At first, like most people, she said, "Of course not. I am perfectly fine." Then, after a period of honest reflection, she said she wished she were taller. We explored the topic together. As gently as I could, I invited her to reflect on how that negative idea that she had about her self-worth had influenced her view of the world and how she related to other people and, in particular, how she related to them as potential and actual friends. She came to understand that she needed to change her focus and attitude. She set aside her concern about being short and started to focus on the many positive things about her and her unique contributions. She applied the reflection process that is the start of the Friendcraft journey and then, using the skills of Friendcraft, began to move beyond her negative, limiting thoughts.

Once she had done that, she saw her way forward. Her inner happiness increased. Her view of herself changed. She changed from being an inward-looking and self-doubting person who judged people by their height to someone who now saw others as individuals. She weighed them now according to their actions rather than as people who happened to be taller or shorter than she was.

Why do we make these arbitrary distinctions about ourselves and then seek to apply them to other people? Why not be comfortable with who you are? Accept your seeming imperfections while being aware of what you have to offer and contribute and then from that standpoint of inner calm and comfort, apply the principles of Friendcraft and move forward as a person and as a friend.

Accept yourself as you are. Be happy with the face that looks back at you in the mirror. Accept that we don't live in an ideal world. Make the most of what you have and therein take a first and most vital step of the journey into friendship.

Let's try another exercise with the mirror. Imagine that you are another person looking at you in the mirror, for this is another key concept that we need to consider in being our own best friend. What do other people see when they look at us? We have learned how we can become happy and more settled and comfortable with who we are and what we can contribute and increase our sense of well-being. But let us now look at what other people see.

What do you imagine others see when they look at you? Do you think you are a person they feel comfortable with? Do you think you are a person with whom they can be friendly? Do you think you are a person who can earn their trust?

My wife paid me a compliment early in our marriage. She said, "I feel as comfortable with you as I do an old slipper with a hole in it." She pointed out that this implied a liking and respect and drew the parallel with a much-valued and loved object. Are we showing the world that sort of persona?

What I am talking about is the face we show to the world, how we project ourselves. Having become our own best friend, how do we then demonstrate this to others? That is the second part of this process. I truly believe that if we are our own best friends, that if we do respect ourselves and our own unique contributions, it will show. We can demonstrate it in how we live our lives, in how we relate to other people, in the positive choices we make, with whom we engage, and how we engage with them. These are all positive and life-affirming choices that the model of Friendcraft and the philosophy that lies behind it are based upon.

Let us just consider how we demonstrate to others that positive essence within us. Nobody is suggesting going around grinning like a fool. There are some situations in which such behaviour would be wildly inappropriate and could lead us into a great deal of trouble. For example, should we turn up to a funeral doing this, people may become hurt and offended. We demonstrate our positive attitudes about ourselves through the choices we make. If we feel we are special and unique, we put thought into whom we admit into our closer friendships. We would not casually admit people who are unknown to us, nor would we be revealing things to them that are in our best interest not to share. We would also want to engage with people who responded to our ideas, who responded to our unique contributions, and with whom we formed a connection, even if that was only for a brief time.

There will be people in life with whom we will form connections. They will respond to us and to our positive attitudes in ways that will become a beacon to us in our journeys into friendship. For example, I once met a most holy man, a vicar in the Church of Wales, who as a young miner had been blinded in a most tragic accident. When he met his future wife, a fashion model, he could not see her; he will never see her. But he heard a quality in her voice and sensed it in the gentle and calm way that she responded to his questions. Through this, a connection was made. And this gentleman and lady over the course of time developed a friendship that blossomed into love. When I said to this man, "You have a most beautiful wife, Sir," he answered, "I hear her voice. I have touched her soul. I know. I do not need to see her face."

Now, such deep and truly intimate relationships are not going to occur in our lives all that often, but there will be many rewarding levels of friendship in which we can engage. The start of it all is to show others we accept and value ourselves, that we are our own best friends. We show this to others through our acts, through our speech, through the choices that we make and the friends with whom we engage, and through the way we engage with them.

For example, we would not want to engage in a destructive relationship. Have you ever been in a situation where when a group of people are together and somebody leaves the room, everybody else starts to talk about that person and assassinate his or her character in every way they possibly can or, as we say in England, pull them to bits? "Oh, she is dreadful, she is. What a shock. I am glad I don't have to work with her full-time. How in earth did we get stuck with someone like that? Have you heard the latest about her?" And so people tittle-tattle. Then the person comes back into the room and it's "Hello, how are you? Have a cup of tea." You see false smiles and forced jollity. This is the very antithesis of true Friendcraft.

I go to an association where people who do not like or respect me come up and greet me as if I were their long-lost brother. I judge that greeting in the spirit in which it is given, and I file those people in their appropriate place in my life.

I leave you to judge where that is. I recommend that should you greet someone warmly, let your warmth be real, let your smile get as far as your eyes. There are people with cold, dead, calculating, or angry eyes who smile warmly, but it is bleak midwinter when you look them straight in the eyes.

Let your smiles get as far as your eyes. If you don't mean it, don't smile. If it is a professional greeting, let it be a professional greeting or a courteous greeting…or even a cold greeting. We don't have to engage with people as if they are all our lifelong pals. Why not reserve that for our lifelong pals? We can always increase the warmth in our voices and our manners when it is appropriate. Why be false? Why embrace the charade and trickery that is so prevalent in modern life? Why not be one who embraces the philosophy of a Friendcraft greeting, which is honest?

I want you to imagine that you are standing in front of a mirror. Look at yourself. Consider the person who is looking back at you. Don't think for one minute about whether this is a face others like. We are not concerned with impressing and influencing people. I am concerned with you. I am concerned with how you see yourself.

Look at that face. Look deep into your own eyes. What do you see there? Is this a person whose friend you would like to be? Is this a person you like? Is this a person with whom you feel comfortable? There are so many people in the world today who do not like themselves. They do not like aspects of their personality. They do not like aspects of their body. They do not like their situation in life. They are dissatisfied with everything that makes them who they are.

One of the most fundamental things in the journey of Friendcraft is to be a friend to yourself, to actually be able to look in that mirror and say, "I like that person. I am at ease with that person. The person looking back at me is a person I feel comfortable with."

People have an almost uncanny knack for measuring themselves against superficial and transitory things in life that actually mean nothing. They are as fleeting as mist and miasma on a mountain slope around dawn. They will dissipate and vanish like wraiths into the night, leaving true reality behind them.

Do not be led astray by such false and meaningless illusions. You are a unique person. You came into this world as a one-off. Your being here is of vital concern to you. You have a choice about what you do with your life. You have a choice about what you think of yourself. These things are not cast in stone. You can make choices.

Some of my colleagues in America would say if it is not perfect, make it better. Get your teeth fixed. Get some hair dye. They go on and on.

Now, this is not a necessarily bad thing. If it makes you feel good, fine. If it helps you be a good friend to yourself, spend thousands on cosmetic surgery. But the person inside all the sticking plaster and poly-filler and all the glue and wallpaper paste and smoke and mirrors, that person is you. There is no plastic surgery for the soul. You are you, however you look.

A good, true friend will not be attracted to be a friend to you because you look a certain way. Now, if you are setting out to superficially attract someone, for whatever purposes, then you may want to look a certain way. You may want to project a certain image. But let's strip away all of that. Let's just think about you as you.

How you look depends on how you are on the inside. I know people who glow with happiness, with confidence, and with serenity. I believe that great beauty lies within all of us, whatever our outward appearance might be. My heart goes out to those people who are so desperate to be things other than what they are, who are so dissatisfied and unhappy with themselves that they do not see their true beauty. They do not see that they are unique and special.

People say that if you are a true friend to yourself, you should learn to live to your potential. I agree with that. We all have the potential within us to make life different and better for ourselves and those around us—friends, family, work colleagues, schoolmates, or whomever. Each of us starts every day with that potential.

Why do we turn from that? Why do we turn to the trivial? We each have the power within us to make our own little bit of the world a place of great meaning, a place of great resonance, a place of great contentment. And in doing that, we are contenting ourselves. In doing that, we are living to our potential.

I once heard an elderly patient of mine start to sing. She was in the later stages of Alzheimer's disease. Her speech had been almost robbed by this terrible disease. But on one occasion, we brought a bunch of flowers into her ward. She looked at the flowers and held them for a while and then started to sing. It was almost as if something was blooming inside her. It was a most profound and moving experience. In that moment, even in the depths of the mind-crushing situation, she let show the potential within herself. She gave those of us who were present an experience that enriched us. This happened nearly fifteen years ago, yet I recall her voice with great pleasure to this very day.

What are we going to do with our lives? How are we going to live them? With whom are we going to associate? How are we going to spend our time, money, and influence? How are we going to regard the people with whom we come in contact? Surely, these are important things to consider in being good to ourselves and being a friend to others as well.

One of the hardest things most people will ever do is to sit down and ask themselves really important questions: Who am I? Why am I here? What am I doing? Which direction is my life taking? Why am I this particular person's friend?

During my life I have never shied away from asking myself those sorts of questions, which is probably one of the reasons why I am writing this book. For example, I was taken by my parents to the seaside at Southend when I was two or three years old. When they walked me to the end of the pier, I then uttered my first words: "What are we here for?"

I repeat this same question to you: What are you here for? I hope that in this chapter I have sparked a few things that will make you say, "I am here to start a journey into friendship. I am here to start a journey into being a friend to myself." If this means asking yourself some searching questions such as whether you should do something about your weight, see a physician, or look after yourself in some other way, surely, my friends, that is something we should all be doing. I urge people to look after the bodies they have been given, and their minds as well. Both are gifts.

Why abuse them? Is there really a good and honest reason for that? I would suggest not. Truth is not to be found in the bottom of the beer or in a casino. Recreation is to be found in those things. I am not against them, but when such things cause you to be any less of a person than you should be, then I say to you, be the person you should be, not the person that society or peer pressure would make you.

If you have reached a stage in your life when you cannot get through the day without, for example, having a lot of alcohol or shouting at your friends, family and neighbours when you are asked to stop admiring your new off-road vehicle, then the tail is wagging the dog and you are becoming less of a person than you really ought to be. If you doubt my words, take a good long look in the mirror again. Would you really want to be this person's friend?

In this chapter, I have spoken about being your own best friend. We have started to see how you can do this and how you can then show this honestly to the wider world, at a level you feel comfortable with. But I repeat my question: What are you here for? And why are you reading this book? What do you want in life, in your friendships? If you aren't happy, why aren't you? What will make you happy? What is happiness? These are the kinds of questions we start to ask ourselves in taking the Friendcraft journey that few ever dare to ask. These are questions that only you can answer for yourself. You know your situation. You know yourself. You know how you treat your body, your mind, and your spirit. I urge you, no, I beg you, to look after all three. They are in your keeping. Please look after them carefully and think honestly and long before you make any choices in your life that would lead any of them to come into harm.

Having considered this question of being your own best friend, we now are going to consider how to make friends.

✪ Activity Four
Getting to Know You

1. What are things that make you special and/or unique? List at least five things.

2. How do you think others view you? Why do you think this? Are there any changes you would like to make? If so, what are they?

3. How do you see yourself?

4. What kind of friend are you to others?

5. What do you bring to a friendship?

5

THE FRIENDCRAFT MODEL

Activity Five
Mapping Your Personal Community

In this chapter, I will share with you the way I have organized my view of friendships. I believe that only by scrutinizing our friendships can we hope to see them for what they are and thereby enjoy them more, while acknowledging their joys and limitations.

We will now consider the types of friendships we have in our lives and how we start to engage with people at the different levels. I like to think of it like an archery target as shown in the diagram below.

THE FRIENDCRAFT MODEL OF FRIENDSHIP

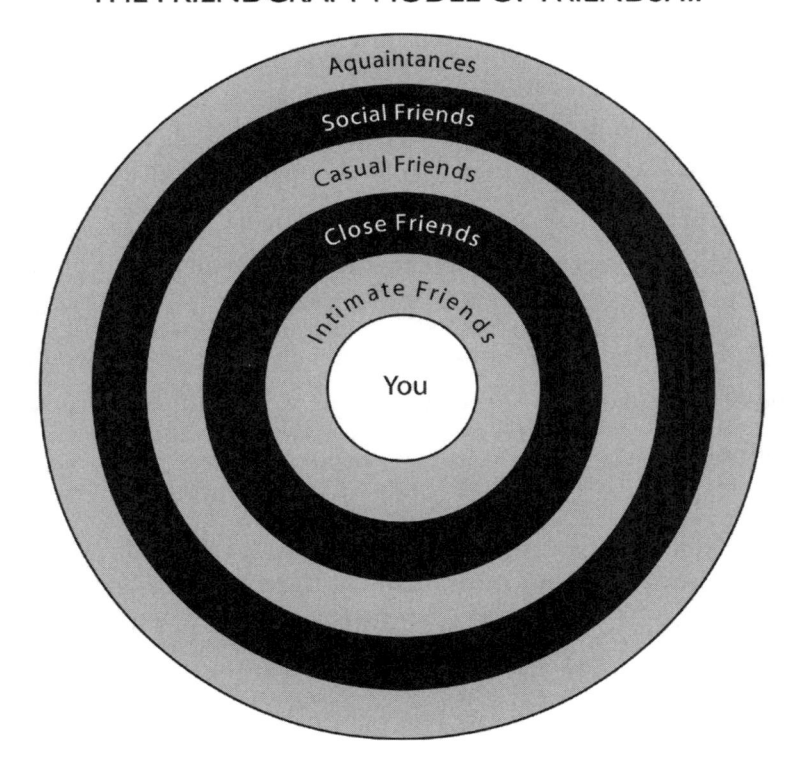

- Aquaintances
- Social Friends
- Casual Friends
- Close Friends
- Intimate Friends
- You

Social Acquaintances

The outer ring represents our social acquaintances. What would we look for in a social acquaintance? Well, we are not going to demand too much. We may just say hello to this person. It may be somebody with whom we have a very superficial sort of relationship. We exchange a few words, a few sentences. We might belong to the same fitness class. We might be in the third row and he or she might be in the fourth row.

Acquaintances may say hello to us as we go in and out of the class. These are people with whom we might exchange a few pleasant comments, or we might even moan along with them. "You know, this class gets worse and worse. It's an absolute disgrace. I have never seen such rubbish in all my life." Just the casual sort of comments.

We would not expect such people to be there for us in hard times. We would not care deeply about them, and we would not expect to share anything of consequence with them. We would not expect such people to know the details of our home life or our family life, other than the few things we choose to tell them. And to be honest, whether they live or die would be of some passing concern to us, but would not be a crucial concern.

I apply the Christmas card test in determining the level of friendship with them. In much of the world at the holiday time, people send out cards, many of them to casual acquaintances, business acquaintances, and friends. Most of them have "Best wishes from…." written inside. We can tell people are closer friends when we write a personal note to them in the card. Our level of friendship and the commitment with these people is greater. I have something like two or three hundred people on my Christmas card list. My true friends on the list probably number less than ten. They get something handwritten by me. The rest just get the standard holiday greeting.

Social Friends

Let us consider the next level of friends, social friends. We have a more dynamic friendship with these people than we have with social acquaintances. These are people with whom we have slightly more in common. We might be on the committee of a club or society with them. We might actually do something with them on a weekly basis. They might be work colleagues who know a little bit more about our home life. They might be people in a social setting whom we have known for a long time.

In England, we have what are known as dominoes and darts teams that play in pubs. We might have people there who are far more than just acquaintances; I would call them social friends. Again, we are not going to expect too much of them, but we are going to demand some level of commitment. If they agree to be there at six with the rest of the gang to play a team game, we would expect them to turn up or to have a good reason for not being there.

We would not regard that commitment as a sacred trust, but it is the first level of an unconscious test of commitment that we give to our social friends. In doing so, we invest a certain limited amount of faith in them. If they do not fulfil their commitments on a number of occasions, we may be quite disappointed in them and consider moving them back to the level of acquaintance to make room for someone we find to be more reliable.

Casual Friends

Some of these social friends can over time be admitted to the next level of friendship, casual friends. These are the people who become keepers of our minor secrets and sharers in our minor joys. These are people who might come and talk with us, and whom we talk to. There are many who come to talk with me at work. "Paul, have you got five minutes? I know you are having lunch, but…" These are people who want to talk to us about their concerns and share things from their lives with us. If we are prepared to engage with people at this level and make the commitment that that requires and they respond in a similar manner, then, at a basic level, a meeting of minds begins to occur.

At this stage of friendship, we are unlikely to confide anything that I would describe as life-altering. Sometimes people will share their doubts and their fears, perhaps about growing children, perhaps about the world in which we live, perhaps about health worries. Perhaps we share hopes with these people, or we invest them with things and confidences personal to us.

We are not sharing the big stuff yet, not the things that if made known might significantly impact our lives. We would not tell them about our deep feelings for another person or our private affairs that we do not want generally known. But we would share some lighter things that are personal to us, stuff from underneath our social armour. These are people we don't mind seeing at times of the day or night when we are not expecting a social call. These are people we don't mind seeing in our oldest and scruffiest clothes.

We don't have to make an effort with these people because we don't need to. We are not trying to impress them. They know enough about us to be impressed or unimpressed. There is no room here for trying to pretend that we are something we are not. They don't know everything about us (who does know everything about someone else?!), but they know some personal things about us.

This is someone we would not mind seeing in our gardening clothes. And if this person arrived, the tea would be put on and the biscuits would be brought out. We would be genuinely pleased to see him or her. Such visits are rarely an intrusion. These people are important to us. They are good friends, but not our best friends. They would know a lot, but far from everything, about us.

If they have a reason to see us, we would be prepared to reschedule some less important things like going shopping or to the movies, but not more important things like attending a favourite niece's birthday party. It would not be a "stop the world, I have to do this" situation, but it would be a "Yes, I am free and can give you a couple of hours in the morning to help you move this rabbit hutch, but I have to do something else in the afternoon" kind of thing. We would invest some of ourselves, but not all. If they were moving and we were free, we might help.

Close Friends

Next are our close friends. We look to them for wise counsel and for support in more difficult times. We look to them to share our joys as well.

A person may not have many friends such as these, and yet this is not yet the most intimate group. These are people with whom we feel especially linked, in whom we confide some of our major concerns, worries, secrets, hopes, fears, and plans. We might discuss a major career move with such people. We might seek their advice about a major relationship issue. And, what is more, we would be prepared to listen to them.

At certain points in our lives, we may need to seek the professional advice of someone who is not necessarily a friend at all, such as a counsellor, therapist, or physician. Some may feel more comfortable discussing these matters within the framework of organized religion. This, however, is not quite the same as confiding in a close friend. Close friends go with us on part of the journey and support us. This is not about paying a fee, getting absolution, or having someone "rattle the bones" at you and pronounce you cured.

We also go to these people in joy. In my experience as a therapist, very few people come to me to say, "I have had a very good year, Paul. Thank you for being in this world." People don't want to see me in their good times. They don't want to remember their problems when things are going right. At the end of the film *The Madness of King George,* the king says to Dr. Willis, the man who had "cured" him, "The king is himself again. You are no longer required, Sir." And off the dear doctor goes into the crowd, smiling and knowing that he has done what he needed to do.

We don't usually tell professionals, colleagues, and casual acquaintances how much we are enjoying life. We do that with really good friends. We might do this with religious leaders to some extent, particularly during life events such as the birth of a child if we belong to a faith that has some form of blessing ceremony for little ones, or on the occasion of a wedding. But usually we don't seek out the clergyman in the street and say, "Vicar, I am enjoying life." In general, we go and see our friends and say, "Life is pretty good." We can relax after a good meal with friends. Let me create a scene for you.

You have just had a meal with some really close friends. Maybe there are three, four, or five of you. The coffee has gone around, and maybe the brandy. You all are experiencing a feeling of contentment, a feeling of "We are all pretty much on the same wavelength."

This is the time when people will actually talk about their secret joys as much as their troubles and heartaches. So if we are going to be sharers of joy, we usually only do that with this level of close friendship and above.

Intimate Friends

This leads us to the innermost level of friends, our intimate friends. These people can be numbered on the fingers of one hand...or, if a person is very lucky, two hands. These are the people with whom we would share virtually everything, however dark, light, difficult, marvellous, challenging, or whatever. They have our confidence and we trust them not only to not let us down but to actively assist us. And if they don't approve of what we are doing, they at least understand why we are doing it.

While I have been writing this book, I have searched my heart many times to set down the philosophy of Friendcraft and its application in people's lives. There are some who would wonder why I have done this, but my truest and closest friends know that I have to do it and understand why.

Friends such as these are in our inner circle, or what I call the Gold Zone. I doubt anyone can have many in the Gold Zone, because a relationship at this level is such an intense thing. It demands considerable commitment on both sides. It is not and can never be just a casual thing. It has to be maintained. You cannot take it for granted.

These closest of close friends, the Gold Zone people in your life, are the people you happily travel long distances to see. You put yourself to considerable trouble for people in the Gold Zone. For good friends outside of the Gold Zone, you may move around a few things on your schedule to accommodate them, but for your Gold Zone friends you willingly go the extra mile.

I was once at a seaside and I saw a gentleman walking along what the British call a promenade, what Americans call a boardwalk. He turned his back on the sea as he was showing off in front of his friends and family. There was quite a heavy swell and a very large wave came and soaked him.

Life can be a little bit like that. A close friend would see that wave coming and say, "Move now or be soaked." An intimate friend might even go and stand by us when the wave hits if he or she thinks this might help us. Plenty of people would run the other way, just looking out for themselves. We will deal with them in another chapter.

What I am saying is that when life events come with overwhelming force and suddenness, our truly intimate friends stand with us.

✪ Activity Five
Mapping Your Personal Community

1. Make five columns or boxes on a sheet of paper and label them with the five levels of friendship: Acquaintances, Social Friends, Casual Friends, Close Friends and Intimate Friends.

2. Think about what would you look for and expect of people in each of the five levels of friendship. Write these in the corresponding section on your worksheet.

3. Make a list of your friends and acquaintances.

4. Write the names or initials of these people under the level of friendship that best describes their relationship to you.

5. Reflect on what you are happy with regarding these friendships and where you would like to make additions or changes.

6

MAKING FRIENDS

Activity Six
Making Friends

If you want to make positive friendships that will enhance your life and those of your prospective friends, then you need to consider your skills at reaching out to other people. You also need a good measure of what a medical friend of mine once described as common sense, "the least common of the senses." In this chapter, I will describe some of the ways in which we can start this process.

Making friends requires good judgment and a measure of trust. Consider the Friendcraft model of friendship with its concentric rings. We tend to start our relationships with people outside the rings of friendship, then gradually work them toward the centre as they become increasingly involved in our lives and we in theirs. We unconsciously set them a variety of tests as they advance inward to the closer levels of friendship, and they set tests for us.

Perhaps you might call this testing "exchanging tokens." Some would call it laying down markers. Some would talk about "crossing bridges" with somebody. The essence of the concept is that we give people opportunities to show us that they are the people we think they are. We give people the chance to prove to us that they are the worthy repositories of our trust. If they disappoint us, we may allow them some more chances or we may decide we do not wish to invest any more time or effort in them. We are both testing the waters. We extend invitations. We engage and test their worthiness and willingness to be our friends.

I am not sure you can go out and hunt for someone to be your friend. You can go out and meet people and engage them. You can put out advertising, including on the Internet, but there is no guarantee of what you will get.

One of the things I will talk about in the deeper level of friendship is the meeting of minds. That could occur with somebody for whom you advertised, but the statistical chances are against it. I suspect you would have to do a lot of searching in that way before you found people with whom you felt comfortable enough to admit to your inner circles of friendship.

We unconsciously or consciously look for people with whom we have things in common. One of the places where friendships start is in organizations where people have common goals.

What tends to happen is that we find ourselves in the company of people of whom we think, "I agree with what he is saying" or "This lady has some good ideas." There is a flow of ideas and conversation that can lead to the meetings of minds, which could lead to working on shared projects and the extending of invitations to become more friendly and involved with us.

One way to find friends is to do things with others. It is hard to find friends playing solitaire. If you spend your time fishing alone, you can spend a lot of time enjoying the river and nature and even meet the occasional fishing person, but you are unlikely to meet many people whom you could look at as potential friends.

On the other hand, if you are in large groups, such as a crowded nightclub or gathering, you are unlikely to find friends, because such places are not conducive to conversations and engaging with others in meaningful ways. You can over time come to know people if you all repeatedly end up at the same part of the dance floor. You may well move on to the more satisfying levels of friendship, but I question whether you would really find true friends in such busy situations if you only visit them on an occasional basis.

Can you find friends at work? Well, there are all sorts of other things having to do with power, status, authority, the system, and such that come into play. Now, sometimes people do make good friends in working situations; however, there needs to be a social element to it. There needs to be an opportunity to really speak to others and listen to what they say. There needs to be an atmosphere in which that can happen, where in fact it is positively encouraged. For the deeper levels of friendship to flourish and become life enhancing, a certain element of trust needs to be exchanged and respected. Unfortunately, that is not always possible in a work setting, at least not with large numbers of people. You would not want your entire office knowing about your secrets and the intimate details of your personal life. By sharing such information with someone in the office or workplace, you take a risk of this happening. If you are going to try to build your friends from people at the office, keep in mind you are not there in a social setting.

What about looking for friends on the Internet and having online friends? Well, I see no reason to discourage people from this, as long as they have other friends as well, but I do caution about some limitations and pitfalls of online friendships. While the written word conveys something of the personality, it is difficult to gauge the true reactions of the recipients of our correspondence. You cannot pick up on the nuances of their verbal and nonverbal communications when you cannot see them. It is also quite difficult to tell the sheep from the goats, the true from the false, and the lurking psychopaths from the true friends. We have all heard the cautionary tales of people who for evil and desperate purposes place advertisements on the Internet and lure the unwary into the liaisons that become dangerous and criminal. I caution people to not become involved in anything of that nature since it can only lead to heartbreak.

If you get into correspondence or chat or e-mails with any person you suspect of having evil or criminal intent, immediately terminate such contact and inform your partner, relatives, parents, or the proper authorities. The first tenet of Friendcraft is to be a good friend to yourself. Your personal health and safety must at all times be of great concern to you and to those who love and care for you.

However, I truly believe that modern methods of communication can be used for good and honest purposes by people of good heart. I know of many such cases and can speak from my own experience that such a thing is possible.

Regardless of how or where we meet people, we look for mutual points of reference that we can build on, because a friendship is a growing, dynamic thing. We probably look for points of engagement more than anything else: "Yes, I know what you mean." "Hey, I thought that too." "Well, I don't think you are quite right there. Have you considered this?" This is the meeting of minds of which we were speaking.

Because friends don't act like nodding dogs in the back of a car and totally agree with each other about everything, there may be vigorous debate between them. This in turn can build a friendship. But there need to be points of positive engagement, large areas you do agree on. Very few friendships are built on constant disputes.

How do we get to a position that we can engage with others in a social setting and actually start to point signposts to ourselves, to open up those bridges that other can cross? Clearly, some people skills are needed to do that. It is difficult to engage others if you are not prepared to speak to them.

You need to communicate with others in a language you both understand. You also need the skills of actively listening to what people say and responding appropriately, to give them the cues to feel confident with you and to know that you are paying attention to them and their ideas. You need to show that you can genuinely empathize with them and that you can help them express those things they want to express. In turn, they can help you express the things you want to express.

There is also the element of trust, of sharing projects, even if it is only having a drink, shopping, or volunteering together. It is about reaching out to others. It is about starting to feel that you can enjoy the company of others in ways that you both feel enhance your lives. That is the essence of friendship.

Think about the levels of friendship I spoke of. In the first level, you are not exchanging that much. In the second level, you tell people only limited things that you feel comfortable sharing with them. As they show themselves to be true and trustworthy repositories of your confidence, then you may progress into telling them a little more.

There is nothing that scares people off more than being told deep dark secrets by those who are clearly desperate. They come across as desperate. They come over as inadequate. They come over as slightly odd and possibly marginally deranged, but certainly as overeager.

Somebody at my workplace would quite casually during the day reveal many things about her sexual adventures that I did not wish to know. Without any encouragement at all, she would bare the contents of her soul…and goodness knows what else…had I not firmly discouraged her from continuing by insisting that discussions about the care and welfare of the patients were the only things that interested me.

And we can be a little bit like that in our friendships, can't we? We can rush around being so overeager in wanting to disclose thing that we fail to notice that everyone is running for cover or their eyes are glazing over and their only thought is "How do I get away from this person?" Do you know people like that?

I occasionally go to social events where many of the people in attendance don't know each other well or at all. As a way of getting acquainted, the people gather in small groups for friendly conversation. Most people understand this is a time for small talk and sharing minor things about themselves, such as their hobbies or pets. Some, however, fail to grasp the value of informal talk. They seem to feel they have to reveal their personal histories and deep, dark secrets about themselves.

At one such social occasion, a group of us had gathered and were sharing stories about pleasurable experiences from our pasts. We were enjoying getting to know each other through this pleasant light conversation when one lady started telling stories about how her alcoholic father had mistreated and abused her from the time she was a small child until she left home as a drug-addicted teenager to get away from him.

This was wildly inappropriate and put everyone in the group on edge. She had suddenly raised the stakes and turned what was a pleasant social exchange into something far more threatening, something far more personal. She exposed herself as being completely and utterly unable to engage in acceptable and appropriate conversation. When it became apparent she would not be persuaded to talk about more agreeable things, people in the group started excusing themselves to go elsewhere.

Do you really think that you would make many friends by acting like that? And if you did succeed in attracting people to you on that basis, do you imagine they would be trustworthy and reliable friends?

I would urge you in pursuing your friendships to look at what you say and where you say it and to whom you say it. Use discrimination. Also, be aware of the clues other people are giving you about themselves. Begin with something small. Don't hit them with your deepest, darkest joy or your deepest, darkest secret on day one. If you do, the only thing you will see of them, if they are like most people, is their heels as they disappear around the nearest corner. People do not respond well to that type of obsessive disclosure or questioning. I would question the motives of people who want to know every little single thing about you on first meeting or in casual acquaintance. This is the sort of thing I would be saying to those people: "What is your game? Where are your questions coming from? You want to know everything about me? For what purpose?" I find that respectful but firm refocusing of the discussion is helpful. Then, I lead the conversation back to generalities or to less intrusive topics.

This is not the exchange of information in the building of a friendship. This is building up a dossier on me, and that is another thing all together. This is when I advise beating a hasty retreat.

I urge people to only be as open as they feel comfortable with being, to be comfortable with themselves, and to disclose as much as they feel comfortable saying and as much as people give cues that they are ready to hear.

If people are talking about their favourite colours, you don't chime in with your experiences at age five or by saying your granny was abducted by Martians. You would be a fool if you did. Go with the conversation. Let it grow naturally. And if you are an overanxious, worried, obsessive sort of person, you might try being honest about it with yourself. If it seems appropriate, you might try saying, "Look, I can come across to people as being overanxious or obsessive, but this is just me."

You may meet someone who is exactly like you and get on like a house on fire. Or, the other person may say he or she is not having any part of that and promptly depart the scene. In that case, you know exactly where you stand; it was most unlikely that you were going to find a friend in that person anyway.

If you mix with people in a social situation in an open and honest way, friendships will find you. But if you feel you must go out and look for them and seek to create them, then I would urge you to be a bit cautious about how you do this. Ask yourself why you feel you must go in search of these things. Are you looking for a replica of yourself? Are you looking for somebody who is different from you, but with whom you have some points of contact? Are you looking for somebody who would complement you by being quite different but sort of fit together like yin and yang, two halves of the same whole? Are you looking for a group of people with whom you can fit into place neatly? Or, are you looking to interact in a sort of a slightly more distant way? Examine your heart. Examine your motives. Then, by all means, go look for your friendships. But I promise you, the very moment you don't think one is there, life will surprise you.

A wise person once said that the measure of people is in the friends that they make. I would say to you that life has a way of rewarding us with the friends that we actually deserve.

✪ Activity Six

Making Friends

1. Think about some of the people skills you have and use when meeting people and making new friends. What are your strengths? In what areas do you feel you would like to make improvements?

2. What are some things that you might do when meeting people to let them know that you are interested in them and open to friendly exchange and conversation?

3. What kinds of things do you do, either intentionally or without thinking about it, that give people opportunities to progress further in their friendships with you?

7

CULTIVATING FRIENDSHIPS

Activity Seven
Deepening Friendships

Let us think of a blade of grass. The most successful grasses bend in a high wind, then spring back into place. Now consider an old dead tree that stands firm and solid. Eventually, the effects of the weather, lightning, and disease will cause the trunk to become weakened and the whole structure will become unsound and break. And so it is with people.

When we have succeeded in engaging with somebody in the way that I described in previous chapters, we then need to consider—and often people do not do this consciously—how we admit them to the next circle of friendship. We advance people from the circle of casual acquaintance through the circles toward the Gold Zone of our closest friendships in several ways.

Sometimes, we engage with them on joint projects and find out more about each other that way. One of the ways to build a friendship is to concentrate on achievable objectives. Take some small steps that can be positively rewarded by success. This is one of the more fundamental principles of the therapeutic process. It is also one of the most fundamental principles of the Friendcraft process. Something as simple as meeting to have a drink provides an element of shared experience, shared expectation, and shared values. By doing this on a regular basis, we begin to know the person with whom we are seeking to form the bond of friendship. We build up a common ground and a fund of memories of shared experiences to draw upon that can help us in planning, consciously or unconsciously.

There are other things we do. Subconsciously, we may give people opportunities to impress us with their willingness to fit into our world. And they will be doing much the same sort of thing with us.

You will be doing this unconsciously in your friendships even now. For example, you do this by setting little tasks such as suggesting an activity you might do together, inviting people to meet with you at a particular time and place, or asking if they enjoy a certain kind of music. But let's think about this consciously, because having an understanding of yourself and having an understanding and an appreciation of the way the process of cultivating and growing friendships works are central to the Friendcraft process. We do not leave the cultivation of friendship to the winds of chance or the blind hand of fate. You would not do that with anything that was important to you. If you own a car, I doubt you would leave it unlocked with the keys in it at night and trust to the hand of fate that it would still be there and untouched in the morning. Our friendships can be one of the most life-enhancing and life-affirming parts of our existence. Why would we want to treat them in a casual manner?

You may want to move people into a social friendship level from a mere casual acquaintance. To do this, you would set them the kind of challenge or give them an opportunity to impress you by their agreement and involvement in a minor part of your life. You might say, "I'll see you next week." Or, "I like your style of coat; where did you get it?"

You are actually asking them something about them, not important information, not vital information, but they can make a choice as to whether they respond or don't respond. People can brush you off with "I don't remember where I got it" or "It was a present" or "I can't make it next week," or they can respond positively and make a firm commitment or give you the information you are asking for.

I once sat in a hot tub with people with whom I was very casually acquainted. We began talking about local restaurants. A recommendation was made, and I tried the restaurant and thoroughly enjoyed it. The next time I sat in the hot tub with these same people, I made it clear to them that I had enjoyed their recommendation, and I made one of my own. The other person tried the place I recommended. He did not enjoy it as much as I did and came back and told me why. We moved on from nodding acquaintances to people who actually talked about a particular subject, in this case food. That is how we progress.

As we achieve the more intimate levels of friendship, we start to set people more complex challenges. For example, we actually talk to them about things that matter to us. On their reply hinges whether we go any further with that disclosure.

I was recently talking with an extremely close friend about the nature of internationalism. I was saying how my views have changed over time. Now, I did not disclose that information to a person I casually knew, but to somebody who had been with me in forming an international friendship organization and knew all the reasons behind it. That was someone with whom I could have the discussion about international friendship and why it should be promoted between individuals and groups of people.

So, the information we share, the challenges we set, become more complex as we move toward the centre of the more intimate and enduring friendships.

But what about when people disagree? Is this Friendcraft model I am proposing all sweetness and light? Well, of course it isn't.

Into every life a little rain must fall. There will be times when you disagree even with your closest friends because we are not robots. And, in fact, it could be argued that part of moving toward closer friendships is actually learning to be able to manage disagreements between friends.

There will come a moment sooner or later in any friendship when you will have to agree to differ on a subject or reach a compromise and move forward. Or it may be that you have such fundamental disagreement with that person that you cannot advance him or her to a closer friendship.

Let us think back to that blade of grass I was speaking of earlier. The grass is a very successful form of plant life because when the wind blows, the grass sways with the wind. It does not break. The wind of controversy, of change, of new ideas, of opposing views, does not break a true friendship. It bends with it and springs back into place. People who are tolerant and can weather controversy and disagreements are more likely to have lasting and varied friendships. They may even pick up ideas, new thoughts, and new ways of thinking from other people.

But there are people who are like the old dead tree that stands rigid and unyielding, who say, "I have the only answer, the only solution. My way is the only way." How long do you think people like that will last engaging with other people? I would suggest that they would stand there like a rock while others rebound off them. I think that person would soon stand there alone, becoming increasingly isolated.

We see people like this in society. They and only they are right. They and only they have the only true revelation and true way forward. Only they have a good handle on everything, and everyone else is completely wrong. Do you think people like that make good friends? Do you know anyone like that? They are so completely convinced of their own righteousness that they are of no earthly use.

Now, we can all be a bit stubborn. I am as stubborn as a donkey about some things. There are certain things in my life that I believe in and that I would dig my heels in like the stubbornest mule you ever met if you asked me to completely renounce them. These are my faith, my loyalty to my country, my commitment to my lovely wife, and my commitment to Friendcraft. But there are many other things that are very much open to negotiation to me.

Friendship is about discussion. Friendship is about negotiation. People can differ about things without resorting to violence and abuse and other things that trouble our world today.

Let us think about if we should stage a disagreement with a friend to test him or her. There are some people who would argue that only friendships that are fired in the forge of controversy will become true steel, the links of a chain that will endure. I am not sure that I would want to create such an artificial situation. I think life itself will provide those opportunities for a friendship to be challenged and tested. I would accept that a friendship can be strengthened by coming through the fire of debate and controversy to a consensus and agreement between friends, but I feel it would be foolish to deliberately provoke that type of experience.

I have a very good friend with whom I do not discuss a certain matter about his homeland. He and I have widely differing views about it, but he is a very close friend of mine and on everything else we are in great agreement. We decided many years ago that we would not discuss this matter. I respect his view and he respects mine. We hammered at each other about this for about ten years and realized that neither of us was going to shift his position. We decided to proceed on the things that united us rather than on the things that divided us. And surely, is that not a way forward for us? Surely, those things that unite us are far more important than those that divide us.

Time and effort are vitally important in growing, sustaining, and developing friendships. Make some time to meet with your friends. Put aside time to listen to what they have to say to you.

How often in this life do we see people who want the instant solution? "I want friends, packaged, wrapped, and delivered to my door! Ready to listen to me, me, me, me, I, me, mine. What about my concerns? What about my life? What about my everything?" These people don't want to engage with people. What they want is a crowd of sycophants around them saying, "Oh yes, you and only you are the important person. I am here for you. I am ready to listen to you."

The desire to be liked, the desire to be one of the gang, the desire to be one of the girls or one of the boys is a basic human desire. From the earliest days, humans have lived in family groupings, in tribes, and, later, in towns, cities, and nations. People nowadays often want friendship to be as instant as instant coffee, but it is not like that.

To enjoy real coffee, you have to grow the beans, harvest the beans, roast the beans, grind the beans, and brew the coffee. At the end of that process that takes time, patience, and commitment, you get a really good cup of coffee.

If you want instant friendship like granulated bean—pour on the hot water and your friendships will be good—I have several thousand bottles of snake oil and am willing for a small fee to show you this Instanto Friendship Oil. I promise you, rub this snake oil on your chests at midnight and you too will be amazed…that I have conned you out of your money.

Ladies and gentlemen…no, let me call you "friends in waiting"…be cautious of those who promise you instant friendship. People advertise that to you all the time. "Hey, I am Tammy. Fly me. I will be your friend. You can do this with no effort to yourself, from the comfort of your own home." Ladies and gentlemen, twenty-five years of experience as a therapist leads me to believe that it is not that easy. I am sorry if that hurts or disillusions anybody, but it just is not.

However, I will speak more about friendship and about ways that we can move forward in building and sustaining our friendships. We want not to magically zap, pow, wow, and suddenly have twenty instant friends, but to find, grow, and develop real friendships with people who will add value to our lives and who will value us for the unique and special individuals that we are.

✪ Activity Seven

Deepening Friendships

1. Think of times when a social acquaintance or friend became a closer friend through doing the kinds of things talked about in this chapter.
   - What kinds of things did you do naturally without giving any thought to how they might deepen your friendship?
   - What things did you do consciously or intentionally with the aim of advancing the friendship?
   - What kinds of things worked so well for you that you might use them again in the future?

2. Think about friendships in your life that you would like to be closer. What are some things you might do that could help deepen these friendships?

8

KINDS OF FRIENDSHIPS

*Activity Eight
Looking at Your Friendships*

In this chapter I will deal with some of the sorts of friendships people engage in and how these different types of friendships can be very positive in their own unique ways. You may want to consider the types of friends you have in your life and acknowledge them for the different contributions they make.

Very few of us could sit down and write out a list of these qualities (unless you happen to be writing a book about friendship or you are of a very analytical turn of mind). But you have an unwritten list in mind to some extent. And in this chapter, I will deal in some of the sorts of friendships people engage in during their lives.

Touchstone Friendships

There are friendships that inspire us in life-changing ways. They are rare, but they happen. I can speak from personal experience when I say that such friendships can occur. And the effects of such a friendship can be found in my life, in that of my friend, and in our wider circles of family and friends.

A touchstone relationship can reach to the deepest levels of a person's being. If you are lucky enough to have this happen to you, you may find yourself making decisions in life that completely alter the path on which you thought you were embarked. These friendships are at a depth of understanding and shared purpose that should never be entered into unless you are absolutely sure that the other party feels the same as you do and that entering into such a friendship does not damage your other previous commitments.

Long-Distance Friendships

There are friendships that are sustained over time and distance. I call them the long-distance friendships. In these days of modern communication and the World Wide Web, it is possible for people to more easily find genuine friendship in different parts of the world and come to know people whom they would otherwise never have met. Do remember my cautionary words about being overeager to engage with strangers whom you know nothing about without informing family, friends, or loved ones. If a long-distance friendship needs to be entered into, then it is important that the persons on both sides are genuine and there is a true understanding of what is involved.

Sometimes through meeting and becoming friendly with people from other places, we can develop as individuals. We can reach out across the barriers that divide us. Some of these barriers are there for good reasons. Some of them are there for no good reason at all. Some are social barriers that our particular cultures or families would arbitrarily impose upon us. Other barriers we erect ourselves based on our past experiences and acquired likes and dislikes. No one should be forced into a friendship. A friendship should grow at the pace that the people themselves set and can deal with.

I do not encourage only long-distance or international friendships. If a person never travels five miles from his or her own home and has two or three good friends there, that person can live a happy and complete life. I have been privileged in my life to know people like that. Two of them I would call personal friends, and I honour these people as much as I honour my friends from other countries.

Philosopher-Mentor Friendships

Another type of friend becomes a guide, a philosopher, a counsellor, not in the touchstone sort of way, but as someone with whom we check things out. Touchstone friends are those with whom we are in such complete agreement and sympathy that we don't need to check anything out with them because we know they think exactly as we do in the vast majority of issues. We are in complete harmony with them. The kind of person I am referring to here—the guide/philosopher/mentor type of friend—is one whom we go to for advice and wise counsel, and this person may also ask our advice on certain matters.

I have a friend who recommended a very good car to me when I was looking to buy one. I didn't want to go for a test drive with a salesman putting pressure on me. I approached this friend and her husband and asked if I could drive their car. They had exactly the model I was thinking of buying, with exactly the features I wanted. I went for a test drive with her. The car basically sold itself to me, but her recommendations as a friend also sold that car to me. It was the recommendation of somebody whose opinion I greatly valued.

There are relationships in life that have a mentor-student type of focus in which the mentor imparts information or guidance or counsel to the student, and the student puts questions and situations and problems to the mentor. The mentor may well answer those or answer by drawing from his or her life experiences. A really good mentor will say: "What do you bring to this session that will help you resolve this problem?"

It is my firm belief that there are no such things as problems, only solutions waiting to happen. If people bring me a particular situation or problem and ask for my advice, I ask them to look into themselves, because usually the answer usually lies there. The role of the mentor is to bring this out.

Purpose-Oriented Friendships

In a purpose-oriented or task-enhanced friendship, people come together to achieve a goal or end. When that goal is completed, the friendship may grow into deeper levels that do not require the presence of the initial purpose or task.

There is an element of purpose orientation in all friendships, but in these types of friendships it is the central keystone, at least at the start of the process. The task at this stage is more important than the team. As time goes on, that alters and the team members become more important than the task to the group.

In the initial stages of this process, people come together in friendship, not in opposition. They don't think: "We are a team, but I am going to get better sales figures than you" or "We are a team, but I am going to get a promotion before you do, you swine" or "We are all friends together, but I am going to go out with that person before you. That person is mine!"

It is not competitive in that sense, although the team may be involved in competition with external sources. Strong and enduring friendships continue among such teams long after the original purpose is forgotten. If the purpose is a just and honourable one, so much the better.

Gangs of criminals want your money, or your information, or whatever. They form themselves in a temporary alliance, and as soon as the pressure is on, they are gone. They will cut and run. Very few career criminals will go back for the wounded man in the way that many soldiers will do. Groups of friends don't tend to leave casualties on the battlefield of life either. They will often go back for psychologically wounded members of the team and shield them. They will hold them in place and sustain them through difficult times.

I know of a group of people who came together in friendship to form a brass band. One of the musicians was blinded in the First World War, a chap named Eli. From that day onward, that band never played from sheet music. They learned the tunes by memory so that Eli would never be excluded from their midst. The band's repertoire was never as large as when they used sheet music, but it was more important to them that Eli was still involved as an honoured and trusted member of the team.

I can think of numerous examples of people who are included when the more cynical and self-seeking would have excluded them. It is a feature of a healthy and properly functioning community that this can happen. People should not be marginalised wherever it is possible to include them.

I have taught first aid to people I knew would never be able to administer it because of handicap or disability. I never turned them away from the classes, because I felt they should have the opportunity to be part of this.

When groups of friends form, it is important that people are included in the purpose. They should feel that they are making a contribution. They should feel that the members of the team value their contributions. They should feel that they have contributed in some way to the success of the enterprise.

All of us have different strengths in life. I believe that you should play to people's strengths, not illustrate their weaknesses and hold them up to them in a derisive or derogatory way, saying, "Look how bad you are at doing this." Rather, let's look in building friendships: "You bring this with you! And that is great!"

Everybody has something to contribute to a friendship. Some people can learn new skills. Some people cannot. Some will not. That is just how life is. We need to work with people as they are.

Social Friends

There is a type of friendship we often take for granted. Those are our social friends, those with whom we just have a good time. But we should never underestimate the benefits of simple pleasure and enjoyment spent in the company of friends. There does not have to be a particular purpose or deep meaning to such interactions. It could just be sharing some laughter and fun, sharing a convivial evening at a pub, bar, club, or each other's homes. All of these things add to our enhancement of life and are part of the unseen fabric that makes our human existence bearable.

✪ Activity Eight

Looking at Your Friendships

1. Reflect on the friendships you already have in your life, particularly those friends who are the most special to you. What do these friends bring to your life and what do you bring into theirs?

2. Under what headings would you classify your current friendships? Touchstone, Philosopher-Mentor, Long Distance, Purpose-Oriented, Social, a combination of these, or something else?

3. What contributions do these friends make to your life? Do you give them enough credit for this?

9

FALSE FRIENDS

Activity Nine
Disengaging from False Friendships

It would be lovely if we lived in a world where all friendships were true, our trust was always received with honour and respected with dignity, and our relationships with others were conducted on a basis of honesty and mutual respect. Alas, that world does not currently exist. Throughout our lives, we will meet special warm and genuine friends. But we will also meet a number of individuals who, using the cloak of friendship, will seek to gain our confidence and in some way betray us at every chance they get. I include this chapter as a warning to my readers. Be on your guard; look out for these people. Do not let the poison that they would bring into your life have any lasting effect.

Drainers

False friends fall into several categories. The first group of these is the Drainers, those who act as though their needs and wants outweigh the rest of mankind's. We all know people like this. They are people who always have had a bad day, people who always have something to tell you about how terrible life is. They are people who, if you are prepared to listen, will talk to you for hours about their problems, their failures, their inadequacies, and how awful and terrible a deal they have had in life.

They will expect you to listen, sometimes to even advise them, but if you would dare to mention that you might have a few concerns…whoa…they don't want to know about that.

They are not there for that. They are there to drain you of all your energy. Some of them will not even know they are doing it some of the time, but they will drain you just as surely as a hot sun will dry up a pool.

Usually, the basis of this is sheer envy. "Why should she have a good life and I, nothing?" "What should she have a good marriage and I am stuck with this bozo?" "Why should his partner be rich and successful and here am I, struggling to cope with this demon of depression or whatever it is?"

You don't notice it at the start. You think for the other person, "Oh, how terrible. Oh, how sad." But think: how many times have these people told you they've had a terrible day? They don't ask how your day was. They rarely start the conversation by asking anything about you or showing any interest about your life. Such people will occasionally throw you a titbit of apparent interest just to keep you engaged in listening to them. This is not a genuine interest in your life or concerns, nor is it motivated by friendship.

In the community I come from we have the greeting, "Are you all right?" The answer is usually "Yes" or some noncommittal remark. It is a noncommittal greeting. A drainer would take this as an opportunity to say, "No, I am terrible. I feel awful." And if the person considers you to be a closer type of friend, he or she can really leech on you for hours. "I have to talk to somebody. You are the only person I can trust. Oh, it is terrible. Oh, it is awful." And every time you see this person, it is always terrible, it is always awful. He or she has nothing good to say.

Praise Seekers

Those who have a need for continual praise also place selfish demands on our time and energy. They have to be bolstered up all the time by their circle of acquaintances. I will not say circle of friends, because these people rarely have true friends. What they want is constant reassurance, constant bolstering up, being made to feel good. "Aren't you the great man! Aren't you the great teacher! The great man is here now. We shall all fall silent, for he will illuminate us all."

There are people like this who have their circle of admirers. They are the stage scenery for the great performer to step forward and tell his or her stories and look marvellous.

I was in the company of such a person a while ago. It was immediately apparent to me exactly what was going on. My heart went out to the person at the centre of all of this who was being led around like a performing bear. Sometimes this circle of acquaintances needs the great performer to perform because it gives them status and meaning and purpose in life. When the great performer moves off the stage, they are left bereft.

Think of the people who come into office with a political candidate. You know, the placemen, the hangers-on, the appointees. When the great person moves off the stage for whatever reason, they are gone as well. You saw these kinds of people in the schoolyard as children, forming around the great athlete or whatever. When that person's star wanes, so does theirs. It is amazing; a very cold wind blows up your kilt, and your so-called friends are gone and you can end up like Shakespeare's

King Lear, wandering mad upon the heath deserted by all except a jester.

I have compassion in my heart for those who have such an empty way of life. And, in twenty-five years as a therapist, I have seen many of them. There is no meaningful and true relationship there. The person has to have the constant praise to keep his or her own self-esteem afloat, and the hangers-on need the great performer to justify their own existence. May we never be like such people, for their lives are empty and they are destined to disillusionment and despair.

Manipulators

Then we have the manipulators, the stage managers of life, the "I am always right and I am going to make sure I manipulate life exactly how I want it" people. Some of these people are subtle. They may appear to be your best, closest friends, but in reality, they are the puppet masters. They are playing you like a catfish on the end of a line. You get just enough line to feel you are running free in the stream, but when they want you, they will jerk that hook and reel you in. There are people who all through life have got to cut a deal, to get the best out of every situation, to get others to do what they want.

There are people who are superb at this. It is their whole raison d'être. They thrive on imposing their will on others. Do not be fooled by anyone who talks about the will of the people. That is bunkum. They are not interested in the will of the people. The people are there to be lied to, manipulated, cheated, and told whatever version of the truth will keep that person in power, influence, or position of authority. Some people will even try to tell you that they only have the true way to enlightenment. But what they really want is to run your life for you.

And so it is in ordinary life. There are people who want the power of manipulation. They are the personal prestidigitators and the mundane magicians. They want to create a world around them where they are pulling all of the strings. If they can suck people into having their strings pulled, so much the better, because that makes even more of a show. These people will make bottles of snake oil appear and disappear before your very eyes. They will convince you that a bottle of snake oil is indeed fine wine.

There are also sexual predators who want to manipulate people into situations that will be favourable for them and less favourable for their partner/victim. A lot of office Casanovas—and whatever the female equivalent is—want to manipulate you because they want to get you into bed.

There are people at work who want promotion more than life itself, and they will manipulate the situation. They will set up situations where they will shine and others will fail. These people are not your friends. They do not want to be your friend. They want you to do their bidding, to be a pawn in their game.

In a hospital where I worked, there was a therapist so desperate to achieve promotion that she would do virtually anything—lie, cheat, steal, manipulate the minutes of meetings—to gain the position she felt was rightfully hers. Over time, her antics became known to the vast majority of the people on the staff and she became a lonely and shunned individual. Few would trust her, none liked her, and many were afraid of her.

She would gain the confidence of new members of staff who had not yet become aware of her nature and she would take their ideas from them and present them as her own. She would give them tasks that were actually hers to do and then take the credit for their work. She would seek to cast others as incompetent or indifferent, and herself as the only person who was truly working for the benefit of patients. She encouraged students to do research for her and then claimed all the academic credit. She had a very superficially friendly and efficient persona; in reality, her aim was to be promoted out of that hospital as quickly as possible.

Gossipers

On the more superficial levels of friendship, some of us can sometimes make the mistake of trusting a person with information that we imagine this person will keep to himself or herself. This information that perhaps is of a personal or embarrassing nature soon is around the office, the club or society, or your place of residence, because this person is untrustworthy or unable to keep his or her mouth shut.

Many people enjoy gossiping. For some, there is nothing like a good gossip for helping the day along. From time immemorial, certain people have thrived on the social interaction of getting together and gossiping about the doings of those not present at the gathering. This is not in itself unhealthy, but when it gets into the realms of pulling people's characters to bits or spreading malicious rumours, this crosses over the border of acceptable social interaction and enters into the realm of false friendship. This is all about knowledge is power: "And I know what is really going on. Mary Jane is secretly going out with Tommy Lee." They are happy to betray you so they can feel important. A moment on the lips, a lifetime on the conscience, except that these folks don't have one. They don't see betraying your confidence as being any big thing. In fact, they don't often realize they have done it: "Oh, I thought everyone knew." And they look around the room as people show shock, horror, and surprise at what they have said. Often, they will come scurrying back to you very quickly to tell you, "They know all about such and such." Well, how do they know about that, then?

I have a method of discovering such people. I will often supply them with an entirely erroneous piece of information with specific instructions that they are to tell no one. Then I wait to see if it comes back to me from another source. Once I did that in a certain hospital where I was working. "Don't tell a soul, but…" And, three years later, I heard that bit of information I entirely invented being quoted on national television.

People Sculptors

There is a category of would-be controllers who pose as friends. I refer to these people as internal sculptors. Over time, they fashion someone into the very form they want for their own purposes. Often, their demands will be very subtle and will be made over time. They don't want you as you are. They want to manipulate and transform you into something that they want in their life. The changes that they propose you make are often internal. Should you become aware that this is happening to you, ask yourself: "Does this person value me as a special and unique individual? Does this person value me for what I bring to this friendship? Or does this person merely see me as a block of marble that can be chiselled into another form?"

This type of person enters into a relationship with the express intent, though often not openly stated, of changing or reforming or in some way altering his or her partner. It is almost like Professor Henry Higgins and Eliza Doolittle's relationship in the musical *My Fair Lady*. One person looks to make the other into something different rather than accepting and liking the other as he or she is. Such people may want their friends or partners to give up their old friends because they feel they are not socially acceptable. They may want them to take up new interests in art or music. They may want to change how the other person looks, dresses, spends his or her leisure time, and so on. They see the person as clay that can be moulded into their type of person.

Sometimes this can be achieved to the satisfaction of both parties. In many instances, however, when the design is revealed, this is fatal to the relationship. This tactic also can be sheer poison to a genuine friendship based on give and take.

Robbers

These are people who want to plunder your intellectual, and sometimes material, resources. They will inveigle themselves into your outer circle, and sometimes inner circle, of friends because they want something you have. They may desire the prestige of being known as one of your friends or hope to get you to introduce them to others of power or position they hope to use to their benefit. It may be that they want you to give them a hand up intellectually or a handout financially. In the most extreme examples, they want to be you.

There was a famous book, television show, and play called *The She-Devil* about a lady who had been supplanted by a particular successful lady author. This author had stolen the affections of the woman's husband. The wife changed herself by cosmetic surgery into the living image of this other woman. She wanted her husband back and so wanted to be this woman. Now this is an extreme example, and a fictional one at that, but there are people like that who want something you have and will go to any lengths to get it.

The honest ones will come as a burglar and just take it. This sounds like a funny thing to say, but at least a burglar makes no pretence. But there are people who will inveigle into your friendship and circle of acquaintances who want nothing more than to have a bit of what you have. These are people to beware of, because whatever you have now they want ASAP. Beware of such people as they are not there on the basis of a true and lasting friendship of give and take. They just want to benefit themselves.

The one common factor with such people is that they want to take from you. A good way to spot somebody who looks like a friend but is not is to ask yourself: "What am I getting back from them?" Friendship is a two-way street. If nothing is coming back, ask yourself: "Why am I doing this?"

This is the test with these people. The Friendcraft approach to friendship is to acknowledge from the very beginning that it is a two-way process. It is also part of our approach when something does not feel right, to take a closer look. Is this a two-way thing or are they false friends in it for what they can get out of you?

✪ Activity Nine
Disengaging from False Friendships

1. Consider the categories of false friends I have spoken of in this chapter. Can you think of anyone currently in your life that falls under any of these headings?

2. If your situation permits, and if you want to disengage from such people, plan ways in which you can be less available to them.

3. Reflect on this statement: To burn, fire needs heat, fuel, and oxygen. Take any one of those three things away, and it cannot burst into flames. If you likewise cut down to vanishing point the opportunities people have to bring their disagreeable influences into your life and friendships, the dark clouds of these false friendships will disappear from your life.

10

BOUNDARIES AND STRUCTURE IN FRIENDSHIPS

Activity Ten
Boundaries in Your Friendships

It is important in making, cultivating, and sustaining friendships that we set boundaries we are not prepared to cross and that we do not want others to cross. These boundaries are not fixed for all time. They may change as the friendship grows and develops or withers and dies, but they are nonetheless there.

For example, if somebody with whom you are barely on speaking terms or whom you barely know were to suddenly turn up uninvited at your house with a gift and attempt to join in a major celebration such as a family party, you would likely think this strange and slightly sinister. You would question his or her motives for doing it.

That person would have crossed a boundary. The behaviour would seem unusual and outside the usual social norms of the societies in which most of us grew up. Very few of us would think how nice it was. Very few, if we are honest about it, believe that people spontaneously run across the road to give us bouquets of flowers. It certainly does not happen in my life often, and I expect it doesn't in others' lives either. There are the boundaries that society and convention set for us. These are boundaries designed to keep us safe.

But we also set boundaries to be crossed only when we give our consent. If people try to do it without your agreement, then they have assumed a level of friendship you have not granted them. Likewise, someone using the art of Friendcraft would not seek to cross another person's boundary until receiving a clear invitation to do that.

It is quite important that boundaries are set within friendship. If there are no boundaries, then the whole thing can spiral out of control, ours or anyone else's, into a free-for-all in which people say and do anything. No true friendship can be built on such an anarchic basis.

If we do not know what to expect of people, and they don't know what to expect of us, then we are not going to build anything that lasts. It may seem very exciting for while, but can you really live your whole life on that basis?

I would venture to suggest that you do not. You build your life upon assumed certainties. For example, if you live in a place that uses electricity, when you switch on a light switch you expect the light to go on or off. If instead of this happening, you sometimes turn on a light switch and get a blast of music or a conjurer appears and performs a magic trick, life would be a lot more unpredictable, even dangerously so.

And so it is with our friendships. We set boundaries we don't really want others to go beyond. When we are mutually ready to cross those boundaries, we advance to the next circle of friendship. But until then, it is important to have our friendships within defined limits. If you have a friendship with someone at work, very often that friendship is maintained at work. If you have a friendship with somebody through a social group, you may not be seeing him or her outside of that group.

I have many such social friendships in my life. I see people at particular organizations. When I am there, I enjoy their company. I talk with them and work with them on joint projects. But we don't expect to see each other throughout the week and in other settings.

If you have very close or intimate friendships, you might well expect to see these people at any time because they have 24/7 access to you and you to them. If you need them, they will be there. If they need you, likewise you will be there. But, again, very few people in anybody's life fall into this category. Such people are in the Gold Zone of your most intimate friendships.

We set some of the boundaries without even being conscious of doing it. These are often based on the baggage and history that people bring with them. All of us have a sum of experiences that makes up how we look at the world and how we see other people. It may well be that we perceive ourselves or others as having certain shortcomings or limitations. We may have reservations about certain types of people, places, ideas, and environments. We bring these with us like a knapsack full of house bricks to every person and potential friendship.

Our baggage from the past can limit us and set boundaries for us. "Oh, I could not possibly talk to her; she is way too beautiful and I am very plain." Or "Oh, I couldn't possibly have a conversation with him. He is way too clever. I have always been quite bright, but I am not in his league." Or "I wouldn't apply for a job there. They only take people who are a certain way, and I am not that way." Or "I would not want to find my friends among those people. They don't look like me. They don't sound like me. They don't feel like me."

These are restrictions that we have placed upon ourselves. You can spend your life being afraid of an imaginary tiger that will leap upon you and rend you limb from limb if you dare to venture down a particular path. But ask yourself this: have you ever seen the tiger? You may imagine you have heard its roar, but have you actually seen it? Let it show itself and then you can make a decision as to what you need to do about it.

Some standards and limits are designed to keep us safe. I would not want people to imagine that they can cross the boundaries that keep them safe in the name of friendship with no consequences. For example, I would not walk into a gang house in New York City and say, "Hey everybody, I'd like to be your friend," because they would say, "Hey, how about this knife or machine gun," or whatever.

If you are being constrained by your fear of other people or your fear of the unknown, these boundaries can to an extent be unhelpful.

Very often, people set up these limits because they fear rejection. They want praise. They are just really unsure of themselves. Part of being your own best friend is thinking enough of yourself and feeling sure enough of yourself that these things don't seem as threatening. Some of the limits that we set ourselves are based on a feeling that we are not worthy to have these people's friendships. We fear an unknown situation because we think we are not good enough or clever enough or that we may be rejected in some way by the people we perceive as being better or different.

Those of us who follow the way of Friendcraft have enough confidence in ourselves and our abilities to see that we have a special and unique contribution to offer in friendship. If our friendship is rejected, we move on. Rejection doesn't crush us. My grandmother used to say there are a lot more fish in the sea, and she was right. We don't know the number of fish in the sea and we don't know the number of people who might enter our lives as friends.

It has been my privilege to know some very handsome men and some very beautiful women. I trained at one time to be an actor. I knew a lady who was considered one of the most beautiful women in theatre. She also was one of the loneliest. She said, "No one will ask me out on a date. They are all scared. None of them think they measure up."

There are people who quite genuinely feel themselves to be disenfranchised from friendship because they feel that they are too pretty, too beautiful, too clever, too rich, too whatever. Nobody should be disenfranchised from friendship for these or any other reasons.

Friendship can find you in the most appalling of circumstances. Some of my relatives in the First World War formed lifetime friendships that began at the bottom of mud-filled trench in conditions that some of us can barely imagine.

Let's think back to what I said about being a friend to you. You are a special and unique person. There is only one of you in the world. You have a unique contribution to bring to this world. You have the capacity to be somebody's friend. I truly believe that. I feel that you can break out of self-doubt, self-loathing, or even just genuine little concerns if you wish to. By all means, have boundaries and limits, but don't let your own perceived shortcomings stop you from finding, cultivating, and maintaining friendships.

There are people out there sitting alone, looking into computer screens, staring at the televisions, looking out windows, escaping from reality by drink or drugs or any of a number of other ways. I know those people exist, because I see them in my working life. I feel their pain and despair.

This saddens me. Those people could have happier, more fulfilled, more worthwhile lives through the power and application of Friendcraft. If I can persuade even one person to turn from that pointless and hopeless way of living and turn around and seize the moment, seize the potential in himself or herself, and experience the liberating power of life-enhancing friendships, then this book will have been worthwhile.

There are people you have never met who would enjoy being your friends. Reach out. Cross those boundaries. Put aside those fears. There are potential friends all around you who are ready to welcome you into their lives.

✪ Activity Ten
Boundaries in Your Friendships

When reflecting on the boundaries you choose to set in your friendships, be aware of the difference between making conscious decisions based on your personal preferences and limiting yourself because of self-doubts and fear of rejection.

1. What are some of the boundaries in your friendships? To what extent are they imposed by your culture, family, or other outside influences? To what extent are they based on your own personal preferences and past experiences?

2. How do your boundaries differ in different circumstances? With different people? With different kinds of friends?

3. What can change these boundaries? Why would they change? When would they change? How might they change?

11

Mutual Support and Effort

*Activity Eleven
Reflecting on Your Friendships*

Friendcraft is a realistic philosophy. I realize that there is an element of shared experience in all friendships. They are not necessarily based on equality, but there will be an element of give and take in all of them. Here are some of the ways people build strong bonds of friendship.

Common Efforts

One of the ways of sustaining and growing friendships is to engage in agreed-upon mutual projects. Joint projects can be undertaken by just two people, or they can involve a larger group. One of the most satisfying things about friendship is actually seeing the friendship benefit not just yourself and maybe one other, but seeing the results of your friendship benefit other people.

There is nothing more satisfying to the human spirit than creating something, building something, or helping other people. For example, every December, I am a Santa Claus at a steam railway. I do this with three or four other people who come along as elves or helpers. We bring joy into the hearts of many children of all ages.

We have a marvellous time doing this three times each holiday season. It strengthens and sustains our friendships. There are people there whom we see only at that time of the year. There are people and families who come back year after year. In a way, we have become friends with them. We have seen their children grow up. They will speak to us ahead of time to inquire if we will be there, and we share special words with them, their children, and, as the years have gone on, their grandchildren. This is an example of a joint project.

If you saw the film *Witness*, you may remember the way the Amish raised a barn together. I have known of projects where people have refurbished houses as a group.

Each year, I join others in my community to create a work of folk art known as a well dressing. Well dressing is custom that has been practised in the Peak District of England for hundreds of years. Wells are decorated with pictures and designs created with flower petals, leaves, and other natural materials. These well dressings take a week to make. We come together and create something that is beautiful and admired by thousands of people. That in itself is a great reward, but the friendships that have grown up over the years during that week are strengthened and deepened by the common purpose and effort.

Mutual Reward

One of the ways to sustain and to grow a friendship is to mutually reward one another. This might be in ways as simple as exchanging a greeting or a smile, and looking pleased to see your friends. How many of us want to walk into a room to see a friend of ours and be greeted by a scowl or a grimace or unwelcoming comment?

I meet with a couple friends every now and again, and when we meet, hands go out like the three musketeers, each hand on top of the other. We light up in each other's company. This is one level of mutual reward.

There are more tangible things that reward us, such as exchanging greeting cards, giving presents, and taking time for each other. We reward each other with the things we say and by listening. We like to hear, "Yes, I would like to listen to you and hear about things you have been doing." Genuinely praising others' efforts and accomplishment is another way of rewarding people.

A friend of mine makes homemade wine. It was lovely to go to his house a few weeks ago with my wife and another friend and his partner. We all sat down and had a meal together. This friend recently retired from work and is learning Chinese cooking. He cooked an entire meal out of a recipe book, a skill he has learned since retirement. It was lovely to see the simple joy when we gave him the great reward of complimenting him, saying, "This is marvellous. Can we get the recipes? Can we do some more? Where can we learn to do this?"

He was grinning like a Cheshire cat. He was walking a foot above the ground by the end of that meal, and rightly so, because we as his friends had gone along to support him. We were saying to him, "All right, you have retired from work, but your life is not over. What you did for your work did not define you. You are our friend. We want to spend time with you even if we are not at work together. We want to come and see you. We admire you for learning a new skill."

What a great meal it was and what a great friend he is. What a great time we all had together.

Support in Hard Times

Earlier, we discussed the life-enhancing power of friendships when approached through the Friendcraft model. We have assumed that with the exception of malicious people, your life is spent in a relatively positive vein. But we now inevitably come to those parts of life when the sky is darker and the storm clouds cover. To each of us in turn will come trouble, doubts, fears, and despair. In each life, there will be moments when you wonder if it is really worth getting up in the morning.

What does a true friend do in those circumstances? Let us think carefully about how we support our friends, because surely there are two ways to go here.

It may well be that a good friend will take time to sit and to listen, to empathize, to advise, to at least intellectually share the problem and give support.

When my father was dying, two of my best friends took me out for a drink. We sat there in total silence for about half an hour because I had nothing to say. They did not need to speak; neither did I. They were also both good friends of my father. They knew how much my father's death was going to affect me. They knew there was nothing that could be done to stop it from occurring. The sands of his life were draining away. They also realized I could not remain at the hospital indefinitely.

And so we sat in the firelight of an old English country pub and just sat in silence a while and then spoke about the many things about my father that we all admired. And, yes, I will honestly say that we all cried together. There was an emotional catch in all our voices. That to me was one of the most supportive moments in my life. Their friendship is something I will treasure until I pass away.

Let us contrast such support, because it may be that that type of really close support is not needed. It may be that a good friend would merely inquire how you are and if there was anything he or she could get for you. It might be practical assistance, time to talk, time to be silent, any number of things.

There is another side to this. These are the people we talked about earlier who appear to be friends but who are not. What they want to do is wallow in their own misery and keep this up forever and a day. Every time you see them, they are harping back to "Oh, it's a terrible life since I have lost my father." They make this an excuse.

There are some people who have seen military service who feel the world owes them a living because of the experiences that they have had. There are some people who have been in a major accident and feel that the world owes them a living because of the trauma they say they have suffered.

There are some of us who have worked in mental health who have seen terrible things or have had terrible things done to us. I can remember one occasion when a drug dealer poured petrol over my hand, saying that if I dared to visit his grandmother again he would set fire to it, that the next time I saw him the match would be lit.

Now, I could spend my life wailing and moaning about this, claiming compensation, and saying that I am emotionally traumatized, but life is too short for this kind of thing. Let's talk turkey. If the bullet misses you, it misses. If the match is never struck, your hand is not on fire.

If you are going to spend your life moaning and groaning to everyone around you, saying, "Aren't I having a hard time? You are going to suffer with me," I say to you truly that you will not have many friends and you will not be a good friend to yourself or to others.

I am sorry if that sounds harsh. I don't mean it to be; however, think on. Do you really want to spend your days listening to people moaning and groaning and carrying on?

In the book *Cold Comfort Farm,* there was a character called Great Aunt Ada Doom. Everyone had to do what old Great Aunt Ada Doom said because she once saw something nasty in the woodshed. Well, we all know a lot of Great Aunt Ada Dooms. Think carefully whether you mutually support each other. Would he or she genuinely be there for you? Or is this person little more than a leech draining your goodwill, resources, comfort, and care and giving you nothing back? Is that truly friendship, or is that in fact little more than sucking away and replacing nothing?

Mutual respect is a key factor in friendship. Support must be mutual. It cannot always be one-sided. Health professionals and religious leaders are there to do the one-sided stuff. That is their vocation. That is what they are paid to do. I am one of them. I sit for hours and listen to people moaning and groaning and expressing genuine concerns about terrible things. I am paid to do that. I can walk away from that at the end of the day.

Yes, it troubles my soul at times. Yes, I have heard some terrible things in my professional life, but that is my job. This has nothing to do with friendship. You do not have to be someone's therapist just because you are his or her friend. You don't have to hire on as someone's permanent 24/7 on-call counsellor because you are his or her friend. There are professionals to do that sort of thing, and it may be unwise for you to try. The burden after a while will become intolerable and you will turn around and say you can't take it any more.

And what will happen to your friendship then? That person may make a good recovery and, as a friend, you may have a very positive part to play in his or her return to normal life. But if your friendship has broken down due to the burden that was placed upon it, where will you be? My advice is to leave therapy to the therapist and friendship to the friend.

Support should be based on a mutual respect that springs from your own understanding that you are a special and unique person and you can help up to a point, but that there is a limit to what help you can offer to people.

Mutual Respect

A friendship should be based on mutual respect, which means you don't go in and advise somebody unasked on how to run every and/or any aspect of his or her life.

Have you ever met people who, when they become your friends, say, "You are doing it all wrong! I know how to do this. Trust me. I have done this before."

The world is full of experts and people who know everything. The world is full of people who are very good at advising others what to do in their lives. But if you looked a bit carefully at their lives, you might find a lot more shreds than patches.

People do ask me for advice in many walks of my life, but if I go to have dinner at somebody's house, I am not there to advise them. If I am sitting casually on the sofa with groups of my friends, I do not turn it into a question-and-answer session about the concept of friendship or start giving people advice about how to do anything.

People who want to do that sort of thing I classify as bubblegum gurus. "I have the instant fix. I know what is wrong with you; I can put it right in just a second." They are just one step away from snake oil salesmen, aren't they? They are not trying to sell you anything, but they waltz in and say, "You don't want to do it that way; you want to do it this way." Well, not necessarily.

You are perfectly capable without Herb from next door coming around and saying, "Oh you don't want to do it like that; do it like me" or Sally from across the street who says, "Oh, you don't want to have that dress, have this one. It looks so much better on me." I would say to them, "Yes, your way works well for you; my way works well for me. Try looking at it my way."

There is an old joke told about gurus. How many gurus does it take to change a light bulb? One…but the light bulb has to really want to change. In other words, if people don't invite your advice, they probably don't want it and it would likely be a wasted effort or even counterproductive to give it.

✪ Activity Eleven
Reflecting on Your Friendships

1. Think of your friendships and evaluate them in terms of: a. time invested, b. loyalty shown by and to you, c. satisfaction overall with the friendship, d. your investment of trust, and e. room for development.

2. What things did you do together that helped these friendships grow and develop?

3. What are the rewards you get out of each of these friendships?

4. What do you bring to these friendships and what do these friendships "cost" you in terms of time, resources, and giving of yourself?

12

Community and Belonging

Our Place in the World

Human beings have a need to belong. From very early childhood, the majority of us have this innate sense of something bigger than ourselves. It is a tribal instinct that has been passed down to us from prehistory and times of the caveman. We have refined this desire to belong. We don't just walk along to the nearest Wal-Mart or supermarket and say, "Let me in. I want to be a checkout girl. I want to belong here." We actually look for what we want to belong to. We look to create and sustain our personal community. Part of what we want to belong to, part of what we give our allegiance to, is predetermined. We are born in a particular country. We are born into a particular race and a particular gender. We have no say over these things.

Irrespective of the things that are chosen for us by the hand of fate, we can make choices about where we want to belong and where we feel comfortable about belonging. These are choices that we make as we grow older. We can choose with whom we associate, where we belong, and with whom we belong.

We look for people who share our same values. We look for people who will accept us. It may be that they demand of us to make some changes to join their group of people, and if that is the case, we need to decide if making those changes is a price we are willing to pay.

If to join the XYZ group of people, I need to shave off my hair, paint my face blue, and run around shouting "I am a teapot" in the middle of High Street, I may decide these are changes I do not want to make. On the other hand, for some people it may fulfil a life's ambition.

However, usually the choices are not so extreme. Usually we can find a place where we feel we belong, where we are accepted, and where our special and unique contribution is valued.

Circles of Friends

Forming circles of friendship is another way to build our personal communities. A circle is a group of individuals, usually not more than ten, who share some of the same ideas, beliefs, and ways of thinking.

People tend to naturally gather in small groups of friends. But where such groups don't exist, we can intentionally create them. But what are the qualities of successful circles?

First, there is a mutual respect among the members of the circle. It helps to have somebody who coordinates the activities of such a group. There is an expectation that all people in the circle will make a contribution. That is not just in money but in time, in ideas, and in respect of the other people who are there.

We want to see that friendships in the circles grow as the members work together on tasks or projects and share interests and leisure activities. For example, if you have a cooking circle, it may be that people meet on a fairly regular basis and everyone brings a dish. Or someone gives a demonstration and you all talk about it. Or it may be that people have a particular interest in a topic or hobby. Being a member of a circle gives us a sense of belonging.

Rediscovering the Lost World of Community

I want to speak to you of a place that is almost lost, of a lost world of community. Not of a particular time, for this is a community of the heart. Not of a particular country, for this is a community of the mind. Not of a particular system of belief, for this is a community of the soul. This world is a place where people can come together in friendship, in mutual respect, where people can support each other not because they feel obliged to but because they want to.

It is a place deep within the hearts of all of us, where somebody would open a door for someone and hold it open as a matter of course. It is a place where we could go to a meeting and feel welcome and actually want to be there. No one is trying to sell us anything. No one is trying to convince us of anything or manipulate us in any way. People just smile, laugh, and want to share time and have fun together. Having fun with a purpose was the place, the time, and the everything in this world.

This world still exists. This world exists in the hearts of some of us. It has never gone away. All the concrete or asphalt, all the lies, hatred, bigotry, and technologicalization of this planet cannot wipe it away. This world is still there. We just have to rediscover it.

Open your hearts. Open your minds. Stand outside on a clear night. Breathe in, breathe out, and just think what would you like your friendships to be like. Do you really want to have everything picked for you by other people? Do you want to spend your life being manipulated by advertisers, politicians, generals, big business, and those who think they know what is best for us all?

There is somewhere else. There is another place where you can find an oasis of friendship to sustain you on your journey through life. There is another way. By that I mean rediscovering the lost world of community where people are your companions in the journey through life. They offer mutual support and refreshment. This community exists in the hearts and minds of people everywhere, but in the everyday world it is often hard to find. Some of us have opened our hearts to it again. Some of us have dared to dream of a time; of a place; of a community of the heart, soul, mind, and spirit where we can in friendship extend our hands right around the world.

Let us say that you feel the need to open your heart to the warmth and illumination to the journey to friendship. Let us say that you are seeking others with whom to journey along that road. Let us say you are looking for an oasis.

The way that we seek to do this is to form groups or fellowships of those who dream the same dreams and share the same interests. Taking the journey entirely alone is a hard road to travel because friendship is about finding relationships and mutual support, being with people in good times and bad, and working on things together. It makes sense to journey along that road with a group of friends. It makes sense to meet with people who share the same desire as you to journey along that road to illumination, the illumination of friendship.

In your friendships, you can choose with whom you travel that road. You do not have to have your friends picked for you. You do not have to have your life scripted and organized for you.

Your personal community can begin with a handful of others of like mind and spirit and grow from there. It may start as a group that meets for mutual support, to enjoy good times, or to work on a joint project. We spoke of the great rewards that come from these things. We talked about supporting and rewarding each other. We have spoken in previous chapters about the warm, comforting feeling that you get from knowing that when you walk into the room, the people there will be pleased to see you.

Imagine walking into a place with people like that after a hard day. It is better than all the health spas in Virginia. It is like having a Jacuzzi in your mind. It is like having Champagne in your soul. You meet with your friends, people who understand you and where you are coming from, who are taking that journey together with you. Isn't this something we all want and can benefit from? If this is not already a part of your life, why not put Friendcraft into action and make it a reality for you?

Real life is about real people. We are human beings. We are not cyborgs. Technology is a marvellous tool, but it should not rule our lives. Open your hearts to real people. Open your hearts to friendship. Open your souls and minds to illumination and refreshment. Why just stare into the screen? Start to engage with other people who are also searching with all their minds and hearts for others who will help them on their journey through life. I honestly believe that we are here to help people find the friends they do not yet know they have. Those friends are there. They are only just waiting for you to take that first step of friendship and you will meet them.

The Next Step

Thank you for reading this book. I hope you have found it both pleasurable and thought provoking. Pleasurable because it is my aim to increase your happiness by giving you the opportunity to think about your friendships and how by using the Friendcraft way you can develop them to become some of the most useful and satisfying things in your life. I also hope it has started you thinking about this whole question of friendships and about the question of happiness.

Many of my readers ask me: Where do I go from here? The answer to that is a very personal one. You may wish to reflect on some of the things you have read in this book and apply them in your life. You may use some parts of this book and leave others.

If you would like to explore the Friendcraft Way in greater detail, there are opportunities to do so. The Friendcraft Institute is arranging a series of courses, lectures, seminars, and retreats to explore the ideas of the Friendcraft Way as it applies in many areas of people's lives, not just in their friendships. I would be happy to provide you with more information about these activities.

There is also the possibility of becoming a part of the Friendcraft Fellowship, which is a group of people who are meeting on a fairly regular basis to study the Friendcraft Way and how they can apply it within their lives to their benefit of their families, communities, and society in general.

If you would like more information on any of these matters, I invite you to contact me at Paul.Barrass@friendcraft.org or to visit the Friendcraft Web site at www.friendcraft.org.

About the Author

Paul Stuart Barrass has spent more than twenty-five years in the British National Health Service as a mental health and personal development professional. Currently, he works with patients and carers and develops programs that demystify subjects such as dementia, coping with change, leadership skills, and personal development.

He enjoys reading, steam railways, historical studies, and meeting friends old and new as he travels about, teaching and writing about the Friendcraft Way.

He and his wife, Shirley, and their Jack Russell Terrier live in Derbyshire, England.